The Invisible Water

From
Leeku's Environmental
Observation Book Series

Mastewal E. Ademe

*There is Massive Water
Transfer Without Our Notice
Before Cloud Formation*

*Harnessing nature's wisdom is key to
securing a thriving future.*

*Invisible processes have visible
impacts; water and community power
can drive change.*

Sustainable living begins with understanding the water cycle.

Tiny vapors lead to tremendous rain, likewise everyone can be part of the solution.

Protecting resources, empowering communities, and transforming the future requires collective effort.

Read this book to explore and figure out our roles thereby producing more food, solving water scarcities and improving climate.

Preface

Explaining every part of the water cycle all at once can feel overwhelming. That is where Leeku's method comes in; he breaks down each piece of the water cycle, exploring one process at a time, making it easier to understand and act upon. It is an effective strategic approach.

This book focuses on a crucial yet often overlooked part of the water cycle: **Invisible Water,** the vast amount of water transferred from land surfaces into the atmosphere. This water, known as evaporation, escapes unnoticed from both land and water bodies, contributing to cloud formation. Many people see rain as a natural gift, without asking how it happens or whether we can use it more effectively. But understanding these invisible processes is essential for sustainable development and solving climate challenges.

In Leeku's village, two big problems stand out: an economic and environmental crisis. Because the community depends on rain and the land for food and water, Leeku is determined to find ways to improve how these resources are managed. He regularly shares his discoveries with others through his **Environmental Observation Book Series**. His goal is to uncover hidden barriers to development while offering solutions to reduce the effects of climate change.

Leeku's family once thought rain came and went without needing much thought. But they soon realized that learning how to manage rainwater could be a powerful way to fight poverty, drought, and hunger.

Every evening, Leeku gathers his family to share what he has learned and spark discussions about new environmental ideas. Over time, these meetings have become an exciting routine, bringing the family closer and helping them work toward sustainable solutions.

Leeku's father believes that understanding nature's processes is a responsibility given to all of us. Although nature provides everything we need, it is up to people to manage these gifts wisely. Despite these lessons being absent from most school curricula, Leeku's family is committed to learning, growing, and inspiring change within their community.

With Leeku leading the charge, the family is not just talking about rain management, they are putting it into practice.

Leeku has discovered one of the hidden reasons behind poverty: the loss of water that evaporates from the land and escapes unused. He wonders why this issue has not been a priority for the village and begins to uncover other hidden obstacles that must be addressed to improve food production and protect the environment.

Some of these challenges include:

Lack of continuous learning: Many villagers struggle to adapt to new ways of thinking or learn about hidden environmental processes.

Skills and labor inefficiency: Farming practices need to evolve to become more efficient.

Poor time management: People are unable to meet the growing demand for food, water, and housing due to poor planning.

Neglected rainwater management: Rain, which could replenish groundwater, rivers, and springs, often goes to waste.

Soil erosion and nutrient loss: There is little effort to prevent soil erosion and improve soil fertility through organic methods.

Failure to recycle soil nutrients: Many farmers do not know how to reuse organic waste to restore the soil's health.

Leeku's mission has grown beyond personal curiosity into a quest to solve the pressing environmental challenges his village faces. He wants to ignite conversations that build awareness about the invisible processes behind rain, the role of forests, and the impacts of climate change.

By connecting the community to these insights, Leeku aims to inspire collective responsibility and action. He envisions a village where knowledge-sharing leads to practical solutions: better water management, soil conservation, and sustainable farming practices.

His father, recognizing the value of Leeku's discoveries, is equally driven to expand this vision. He dreams of creating a network that includes local organizations, schools, churches, farmers, and youth groups to establish a common understanding of their environmental responsibilities.

Together, they can design sustainable initiatives that protect their resources and climate. With a shared commitment, they hope to build resilience against climate change, improve their agricultural yield, and inspire nearby communities to adopt similar approaches.

The environment operates on universal principles that connect ecosystems across the globe. This shared blueprint means the strategies in **The Invisible Water** can be applied in diverse landscapes, from arid regions to rainforests. By adapting these foundational water management practices, communities anywhere can foster resilience, support sustainable agriculture, and create harmony between human needs and natural systems. Embracing these principles benefits not only local ecosystems but also contributes to global environmental stability.

Therefore, sharing this book with developing countries is not just beneficial but essential. By providing access to these insights, communities can better understand and apply sustainable practices tailored to their unique environments. This knowledge exchange can drive meaningful change, empowering individuals to manage resources more effectively and contribute to a healthier planet.

Introduction

Scientists identified that water in the air plays a critical role in regulating our planet's temperature. When clouds cover large areas for extended periods, they help cool the Earth by shading sunlight. However, climate change can disrupt this balance. Heavy clouds may sometimes trigger floods and hurricanes. On the other hand, prolonged dry spells without cloud cover increase the risk of droughts and wildfires.

The air around us contains moisture, even when we cannot see it. A simple way to observe this is by noticing how water droplets collect on a cold soda bottle or the outside of a car window when the air conditioning is running. These tiny droplets reveal the hidden water in the air. When the air cools down enough, that invisible water can turn into fog or clouds. Ask a question: can we play a role to cool down the air? Yes, but how?

Teaching communities about these hidden processes is essential for improving agriculture and avoiding poverty.

Understanding how water moves through the air helps people make better decisions about farming, water use, and conservation. When people act on this knowledge, they not only increase food production but also protect the environment.

In one of their evening discussions, Leeku's father asks a tough question: "Why have we not modernized our agriculture like other countries? What is holding us back?"

This question sparks a thoughtful discussion among the family. Despite farmers working tirelessly to bring food to the **Mosob,** the traditional woven table used for communal meals, the results often fall short. Even with all their efforts, many people in the village still do not have enough to eat.

Leeku's father worries that with current farming methods, it will be difficult to feed everyone in the future. While farmers are doing their best, something hidden is limiting their success. Worse, the same processes that reduce crop yields are also harming the local climate, creating a cycle of hardship that is hard to escape.

It seems strange that 90% of the population, who are farmers, cannot produce enough food for themselves and the remaining 10% of non-farmers. Leeku is convinced that understanding and addressing the unseen environmental processes will unlock new ways to improve both food production and the local climate.

These hidden processes such as water evaporation, soil nutrient loss, and topography change are quietly draining resources and contributing to poverty and climate change. But Leeku is determined to bring these issues to light. His goal is to transform his village by solving these hidden challenges, ensuring that the community can thrive while also helping to minimize the global climate crisis.

The Invisible Water

After returning from their journey, Leeku's brother eagerly lays out the arrow-stamped pictures they collected. These images capture the endless process of evaporation, demonstrating how rising heat and shifting air currents carry water vapor from lakes and rivers up into the atmosphere.

"Look!" Leeku's brother points to their picture of Lake Tana, Ethiopia's largest lake. "We saw how the water 'takes off' from the surface through evaporation. That is the first step of the water becoming part of the air, even though we cannot see it at this stage."

Leeku nods, adding, "So, it is time to connect everything we observed. Each tiny bit of evaporated water seems small on its own, but together it becomes huge. It is that invisible movement that gives us the rain responsible for nearly all of the food we grow here in the village."

"Exactly," his brother agrees. "Not only is rain our primary water source, but it is also the cleanest water we get, compared to groundwater or streams that collect dirt and pollutants along the way."

Leeku thinks for a moment. "Clouds do not just bring rain, they give us shade, cooling the air and helping the climate too."

His brother continues: "When water evaporates from the lake, wind and heat start carrying it higher into the atmosphere. We were lucky to see this process beginning over Lake Tana. Even though the water vapor is invisible, it becomes part of the cloud-forming process the moment it joins the air."

"Wait," Leeku asks, "are you saying the air always carries water, even when we cannot see it?"

"Exactly," his brother explains. "The air holds different amounts of moisture depending on the temperature and location. If you combine all the moisture evaporation to the atmosphere, it equals the amount of rainwater that falls worldwide. As you go higher into the sky, the air gets colder. That is what makes condensation possible: the water vapor cools and starts turning into visible clouds."

Leeku's face lights up with excitement. "That is where clouds come from. Last time we know that they start on the ground, as water vapor. Now we learned they rise into the sky where they become visible. I finally understand the connection!"

"Right," his brother says. "Humidity is just another word for the moisture in the air. When air with water vapor cools enough, the vapor condenses into fog, which are part of clouds."

"That is amazing," says Leeku. "The air is like a water-fetching tool for us. But it needs heat from the sun for three reasons: to evaporate water, to create rising air through temperature differences, and to generate wind for moving that air carrying water."

Curious, Leeku asks, "But what if there is no wind? How does the water vapor get high enough to form clouds?"

His brother smiles. "Even without wind, the air carrying water vapor moves upward because of heat differences. The sun heats the surface of the earth, warming the lowlands more than the upper atmosphere. Warmer air rises, and cooler air sinks. This constant shifting allows water vapor to travel upward until it reaches a level where the air is cold enough for clouds to form."

They discovered a fascinating process of water moving upward into the air on its own, without the help of wind.

Leeku's eyes narrow as he tries to absorb the information. "So, the vapor keeps rising until it hits its limit to the point where it cannot go any higher. That is where the clouds finally take shape."

His brother adds, "Sometimes, depending on the season or the altitude of a place, the temperature difference might not be strong enough to create upward movement. In those cases, the air is said to be **humid**. When the air is very humid, you might even see fog forming near the ground."

Leeku takes a deep breath, thinking about what this means for his village. "So, even though we cannot see it, hot air is always pulling water away from the land and that might not be good for our crops. Because crops need water very much to keep soil moist."

His brother nods thoughtfully. "Exactly. When the air heats up, it becomes lighter and rises, creating space that pulls in other air molecules. That is what makes wind blow. But if the air becomes too dry or the wind too strong, it can dry out the soil and harm plants."

Leeku taps his chin. "So gentle wind is helpful for bringing rain, but harsh winds can be dangerous."

"Right," his brother says. "Wind plays a key role in rain formation, but it needs to stay balanced. Both gaseous, like water vapor, and liquids tend to move into open spaces. However, gaseous moves freely in all directions based on temperature differences, while liquids flow downward due to gravity."

Leeku's brother continues by reevaluating: "As the moist, warm air rises, it cools and forms clouds. This happens even without wind because of the natural upward movement caused by heat differences between the earth's surface and the cooler upper atmosphere. The clouds form distinct layers at different heights, and the movement only stops when the air reaches a level where it is too cold for the water vapor to rise any higher."

"So," Leeku sums up, "If there is no heat difference, the vapor stays on the ground. This shows that providing shade to create cooler air near the soil is essential. And if the air is humid enough, we might get fog instead of rain."

"Exactly," his brother agrees. "That is why it is so important to understand these invisible processes. They affect everything from how we grow food to how we deal with the climate."

Leeku grins. "This makes me realize how complex the water cycle is. It is not just about rain, it is about the invisible water that is always around us, moving and working in ways we did not notice before."

Leeku's brother gave him a proud pat on the back, his eyes full of encouragement. "Now that we understand these processes, we can begin taking real steps to protect our water resources and use them more thoughtfully. It is like we have unlocked a key to understanding how nature supports us and with that knowledge, we have a responsibility."

After a pause he continued, "Imagine if we not only made changes here in our own village but also shared what we have learned with others. If we keep learning, finding new ways to conserve, and passing on what we know, we can help our village thrive and even inspire nearby communities to follow our lead. This is more than just a discovery; it is a chance to make a difference for everyone around us."

With a shared sense of purpose, Leeku and his brother began discussing ways to put their newfound knowledge into action, from teaching neighbors about rainwater harvesting to organizing village cleanups. They realized that step by step, they could bring their entire community into a sustainable, nature-aligned way of life.

Leeku and The Invisible Water

"Wow," exclaimed Leeku, "Last time we saw the boat, it was floating on water, and now we have learned that the water evaporating from it eventually forms floating clouds. It is amazing! We can say that **the floater floats** always, in one form or another."

They both laughed, filled with excitement over their discovery.

His brother added, "Oceans contribute the most to cloud formation because of their vast size, though rivers, lakes, and even land surfaces play a role too."

"What are oceans?" Leeku asked, curious.

His brother smiled. "Let me explain. Water bodies have different names based on their size and flow. Flowing water includes springs, canals, and rivers. Stagnant water that does not move much includes soil moisture, wetlands, ponds, lakes, seas, and finally, oceans which are the largest bodies of water, covering a huge part of the earth."

Leeku thought about it. "So, if we did not have big oceans, getting enough rain would be a problem?"

"Exactly," his brother replied. "The oceans are massive enough to provide the water vapor needed for rain to form. Since cloud formation begins with micro-evaporation, we need large water sources to keep up with the demand. Not only that, it needs enough time to meet the required level."

Leeku recalled what he had learned on their journey: "The Sun's heat pumps water into the air, which then travels with the wind created by temperature differences. So, the Sun plays a crucial role in cycling water and mobilizing it across the atmosphere."

His brother nodded. "Yes, the Sun drives everything from evaporation to the creation of wind and cloud formation. Water's ability to change from liquid to vapor allows nature to maintain a continuous system of water pumping and rainfall, without human effort."

Leeku was amazed by how water, air, and heat all worked together in harmony. "It is incredible to think that clouds are actually water in disguise rising invisibly and only becoming visible when they turn into clouds. And from there, they float until they fall as rain."

"Yes," his brother agreed. "And this process teaches us a powerful lesson: that small, invisible actions can lead to big outcomes. Just as evaporation starts small but results in large rainfalls, our community can create positive change through small but consistent efforts."

Leeku beamed at the idea, remembering the first book. "So,

when tiny clouds gather and cool down, they turn into darker, heavier clouds through condensation. When the water droplets get too heavy to float, they fall as rain!"

"Exactly!" his brother said, pulling out a picture they had taken during their trip. "This shows how condensation creates the raindrops that water our crops."

Leeku's curiosity deepened. "Do we always make the best use of the rainwater we receive?"

His brother smiled. "That is a big question, Leeku. we will explore that together soon."

To help Leeku understand more, his brother sketched a world map. "See this blue part? It shows where the oceans are, covering nearly 75% of the earth's surface. The large surface area of oceans is key to generating enough water vapor to sustain global rainfall."

Leeku looked at the map, pondering. "If the oceans were smaller, would rain be scarce?"

"Correct," his brother replied. "The size of these water bodies was designed perfectly. Without their vast coverage, life on earth would be impossible."

"Wow!" Leeku exclaimed. "The Earth's large water bodies are essential for life, just like our small efforts matter in taking care of the environment."

His brother nodded. "Exactly. Just as tiny processes in nature work together for a big impact, small actions by people like planting trees or conserving water can have significant results over time."

Leeku's father joined the conversation, saying, "If each of us does our part, even in small ways, we create powerful change. When a whole community works with the same purpose, the cumulative effect can be extraordinary."

Leeku paused thoughtfully, reflecting on the connection. "I see now why planting trees is so important," he said, his voice filled with realization. "Trees play such a big role in keeping the environment stable. By providing shade and cooling the air around them, they naturally help to reduce temperatures. This cooling effect means that water does not evaporate too quickly, which helps keep more moisture in the soil and the air. With more moisture available, cloud trapping as well as formation becomes easier and more consistent, especially in areas where rain is scarce."

They discovered that condensation is the process where clouds transform into water droplets, and trees play a crucial role in cooling down the local air to support this process. An impressive insight!

"Plus, when trees cool the air, they make it more likely for clouds to condense and gather, leading to gentler rainfall rather than sudden, extreme storms. Without enough trees, we would see more intense evaporation and less control over water cycles. Hurricanes, floods, and even droughts would become more common, disrupting the balance of life. Planting trees, then, is not just about greenery it is about creating stability in the water cycle and protecting our communities from severe events."

"You are absolutely right," said his brother. "Forests cool the air, reduce temperatures, and create fresh air for us. That is why many monasteries are surrounded by trees, having enough water potential. They understand how to live in harmony with nature."

"Walking under tall trees where grass covers the ground feels special, one can feel and breath the cool air," Leeku said. "It is peaceful and refreshing."

His brother smiled. "Trees help create these cool microclimates, which are essential in combating the effects of climate change. When we reduce the temperature around us, we make it easier for nature's tiny processes to keep working smoothly."

Leeku's father added, "Climate change means a disturbance in this natural balance. When too much water evaporates, we get heavier rains, leading to floods and hurricanes. A shift in the water cycle can cause unpredictable weather, such as sudden downpours or droughts."

Leeku nodded thoughtfully. "So, there is always more water in the air than we realize. Even though we only see clouds and rain, the invisible part of the water cycle is much bigger. **The future is bright if we tap this resource using solar energy.**"

His brother confirmed, "Yes, a lot more water is evaporating than what we see falling as rain. However, if this invisible water pumping did not happen continuously, we would face water shortages and life would become very difficult. But we would not allow on land surface for our and climate benefit."

Leeku reflected on the complexity of the process. "Even though the steps seem small and invisible, they are part of a vast system. I think we can learn from this that we need to recognize the value of small actions that add up over time to improve our environment."

His brother smiled. "Exactly. Nature teaches us that consistency matters. Just like the Sun, water, and wind work tirelessly to maintain life on Earth, we need to do our part."

Leeku's father encouraged him: "Study what happens to rainwater after it falls to the ground. The more we understand, the better we will be at managing our natural resources wisely."

Leeku thought deeply for a moment, then said, "The Sun is truly amazing. It is life's energy, supporting everything from food production to transportation, health, and even water recycling. Without it, life would not be possible. At night, we get a much-needed break; otherwise, the relentless heat of the sun would continue evaporating water, increasing the risk of wildfires."

His brother nodded in agreement. "Yes, the Sun drives nearly every process we depend on whether it is warming the earth, creating rain, or supporting plant growth. it is a gift we must learn to use wisely."

Quietly, Leeku reflected on all he had learned. "I see now that everything is connected to water, air, sunlight, and the land. And if we can understand how these invisible processes work, we can take better care of our environment."

His father smiled warmly, nodding with pride. "That is exactly right, Leeku. Nature has been guiding us all along, showing us how each small step contributes to something much larger. When we learn from nature's rhythms and hidden processes, we gain the wisdom to work alongside it rather than against it. Think of the water cycle, it works silently, every moment, even though we cannot always see it. Each droplet of water that rises and falls might seem insignificant on its own, but together, they create life-giving rain, rivers, and thriving ecosystems.

"So, when we take small but thoughtful steps, like conserving water, planting trees, or respecting the land, we become part of that larger cycle. We can bring meaningful change in our community just by aligning with these natural principles, just as the invisible water cycle does every day. Little by little, these actions add up, creating a better future for everyone."

Conclusion

Leeku's exploration and environmental lessons are inspiring! It beautifully weaves together concepts of water cycles, community action, and environmental stewardship, making it not just engaging but also highly educational.

Leeku's journey highlights that sustainable environmental management depends on understanding natural processes, fostering unity, and acting with intention. Nature works in unseen ways also, but with knowledge and community effort, small changes can lead to significant transformations.

The message is clear: We all breathe the same air and rely on the same water cycles. This shared reality calls us to unite for the health of our planet.

Leeku's story offers a simple truth: Everyone can play a role, and together, we can create a resilient, sustainable world.

The Way Forward

Through this series, Leeku has come to understand the intricate natural processes that allow clouds: essentially floating water in a vapor form, to form and travel across the sky. This phenomenon is made possible by the Earth's vast water sources, including oceans, rivers, and lakes. These bodies of water continually interact with the sun's energy, which provides the heat needed to convert liquid water into vapor. This transformation, known as evaporation, enables water molecules to rise invisibly into the air, where they are carried by wind currents as well.

The sheer size of the Earth's oceans plays a vital role in this process. Covering over 70% of the planet's surface, oceans act as a global reservoir, supplying most of the water vapor that eventually condenses into clouds and returns to the land as rain. Leeku's exploration highlights how each part of this cycle is interconnected, with water's unique ability to shift between liquid, vapor, and eventually back to liquid as rain, sustaining life on Earth. The role of the air in this journey is equally significant; air currents not only transport water vapor over large distances but also contribute to cloud formation and the distribution of rainfall.

This understanding has made Leeku aware that the ocean's size and the sun's energy are crucial for maintaining the global water cycle that provides rainwater to nourish plants, replenish rivers, and sustain life. By grasping these natural cycles, communities can better appreciate the fragile balance needed to sustain resources and recognize the ocean's essential contribution to climates and agriculture around the world.

This invisible process of evaporation, while often unnoticed, offers powerful insights that communities can learn from to sustainably manage resources and ensure a thriving environment. In understanding how water naturally evaporates, moves, and eventually returns as rain, we uncover a model of harmony in nature, one that encourages human actions to be aligned with these natural principles. When communities grasp this cycle, they realize that unchecked water evaporation on land can disrupt the delicate balance needed for ecosystems and agriculture.

If water is allowed to evaporate excessively from exposed soil or deforested lands, it contributes to rapid depletion of local groundwater levels. This uncontrolled loss can lead to water scarcity, as there is less moisture available to support agriculture, forests, and grasslands. Over time, this depletion accelerates desertification, reducing the land's productivity, and can trap communities in cycles of poverty. Climate change intensifies this cycle even further, as rising temperatures increase evaporation rates, amplifying these effects and posing a serious challenge to wealth creation in affected areas.

Leeku's new understanding of these natural processes has inspired him to develop strategies that aim to retain water, restore greenery, and optimize rainfall use in his village. He envisions solutions that will not only safeguard his community's water resources but will also create economic resilience and foster a culture of environmental stewardship. By aligning with nature's principles, Leeku seeks to transform his village into a model of sustainability, demonstrating how human ingenuity, when harmonized with nature, can lead to thriving communities and a healthier planet.

Guiding Questions for Future Exploration

Leeku's environmental journey deepens with two vital questions that stand to transform his approach to water conservation and climate resilience:

1. How can we increase cloud formation to ensure consistent rain, even in dry seasons?

In exploring this question, Leeku aims to understand how communities can actively participate in enhancing natural water cycles to sustain rainfall, especially during dry periods. He recognizes that consistent rainfall is critical not only for farming and daily water needs but also for maintaining a balanced ecosystem. His focus will be on identifying practices that could encourage cloud formation, like reforestation to cool the land and increase moisture in the air, improving soil health to retain water, and exploring new techniques for enhancing local water cycles. By studying these methods, Leeku hopes to ensure that his village, and potentially the entire region, can experience reliable rain throughout the year, even in challenging climatic conditions.

2. Are we adequately prepared to manage the rainwater we receive to maximize its benefit?

Leeku realizes that simply receiving rainwater is not enough; it is equally important to efficiently capture, store, and distribute it. This question propels him to assess the readiness of his community to make the most of every drop, especially as climate variability increases. He plans to investigate rainwater harvesting techniques, the use of reservoirs, and effective land management practices to prevent water loss. His goal is to establish systems that ensure rainwater supports crops, replenishes groundwater, and sustains local ecosystems, making his village resilient against periods of drought or water shortage.

These guiding questions will shape Leeku's journey as he works to design practical, sustainable solutions that safeguard water resources for his village and region. Through his exploration, he hopes to inspire others to see water as a communal responsibility and a resource that, with careful management, can transform communities and secure their futures.

Below are some thoughts and recommendations to further work for Leeku's Environmental Observation Book Series.

Refining the Story's Themes

1. Water as a Connector
   - ➢ Emphasize how water connects everything: oceans, land, forests, and the atmosphere while making it clear that every drop of water matters.
   - ➢ Introduce a diagram or flowchart to visually explain how invisible processes (evaporation, condensation, and precipitation) form the basis for all environmental systems.

2. Unity in Action and Environmental Equity
- ➤ Deepen the message about equity by showing examples of how communities that work together like Leeku's achieve positive environmental change.
- ➤ Add anecdotes of successful community-driven projects to inspire readers and showcase tangible solutions.

3. Solar-Powered Solutions
- ➤ Leeku's idea about harvesting invisible water with solar-powered condensation meshes is visionary. Explore this concept with a mini project: "Leeku's Experiment: Building a Simple Solar Still."
- ➤ Include instructions for readers to try small-scale condensation models,

encouraging hands-on learning.

4. Connection to Climate Change
   - ➤ Strengthen the narrative on global warming by showing contrasts: what happens when forests thrive vs. when deforestation occurs.
   - ➤ Introduce brief stories from other regions where reforestation or rainwater harvesting transformed local environments, reinforcing the role of small efforts leading to big changes.

Suggested Structure

Below is a suggested reorganization for to clarify the call to action and next steps.

1. Summary of Leeku's Key Learnings:
   ➢ Water vapor is invisible but essential.
   ➢ Oceans are the primary source of rainwater.
   ➢ Forests help maintain a balanced climate.
   ➢ Nature offers free resources (solar energy, wind, rain) that must be managed wisely.

2. Proposed Solutions & Tools for the Future
   ➢ Solar-Powered Condensation Systems: Use renewable energy to harvest invisible water.

➢ Reforestation Projects: Plant trees to mitigate global warming, reduce evaporation rates, and improve local rainfall patterns.

➢ Equitable Resource Distribution: Ensure every community member has access to water and environmental resources, fostering unity and motivation.

Proposals for Community Action

1. Promote Environmental Education:

➢ Advocate for the inclusion of Leeku's Environmental Observation Book Series in school curriculums.

➢ Organize environmental clubs where students can apply

Leeku's lessons through local projects.

2.   Community   Rainwater Harvesting:
  ➢ Initiate rainwater collection systems at the village level, especially during peak rainy seasons, to store water for dry periods.
  ➢ Conduct workshops on the benefits of rain barrels, reservoirs, and ponds to manage rainfall sustainably.

3. Incentivize Tree Planting:
  ➢ Develop partnerships with local monasteries and cultural institutions to increase forest coverage.
  ➢ Encourage communities to plant native trees that align with local climates to boost

biodiversity and sustain water resources.

4.   Solar   and   Wind   Energy Initiatives:
> Introduce   affordable   solar solutions   for   households, making it possible to power water condensation systems and reduce dependence on conventional energy sources.

The Role of Forests, Climate, and Solar Energy

Leeku understands that community engagement with nature directly impacts resource management. Deforestation not only reduces oxygen supply but also increases local temperatures, intensifying global warming and disrupting cloud formation. This imbalance can trigger hurricanes in some regions and wildfires in others, while accelerating desertification.

He realizes that forests are essential for creating cooler, moisture-rich environments that promote rainfall. Planting trees is crucial not only for temperature regulation but also to stabilize the water cycle.

The Invisible Water: Potential Solutions Using Solar Energy

Leeku proposes innovative ways to manage the invisible water floating above us:

> ➢ Solar-powered condensation systems to harvest invisible water and generate fresh water at key sites.
> ➢ Rainwater harvesting infrastructure to store seasonal rains for later use, extending water availability during dry periods.

These solutions align with nature's design using solar energy and air to generate water sustainably, without the need for costly interventions.

The Call for Unity: Our Shared Responsibility

Nature provides essential resources air, water, solar energy that are fundamental to life. Leeku believes that the path to sustainability requires collective action and unity. Every community member must contribute to environmental stewardship, for it is only through cooperation that we can overcome challenges like climate change, water scarcity, and land degradation.

This journey teaches an essential truth: The smallest actions, when multiplied across communities, can create meaningful change. Leeku reminds us that we all breathe the same air, rely on the same water cycles, and share one planet. It is our shared responsibility to manage it wisely and protect it for future generations.

Nature as a Model for Change

Leeku's journey inspires a simple yet profound message: Small, invisible processes in nature have enormous impacts. In the same way, individual efforts when aligned with natural principles can lead to powerful outcomes. The environment demands thoughtful, united actions to address unseen challenges and foster sustainable development.

The next part of **Leeku's Environmental Observation Series** will explore practical strategies to enhance rainfall, extend water availability, and use nature's principles to transform Leeku's village and beyond. This journey is a call to action for communities everywhere to learn from nature, work together, and create a better future for all.

Some of the published books

About the Author

Mastewal E. Ademe holds a master's degree in water resources management from the IHE-Delft Institute for Water Education, the Netherlands, and a Bachelor of Science in Agricultural Engineering from Alemaya University of Agriculture, Ethiopia.

An expert for more than fifteen years in Soil and Water Conservation. Also appointed as head of water resources management in Ethiopia. Then worked as a coordinator for the Participatory Small-Scale Irrigation Development Program in Ethiopia for about three years. During this period, based on the approach awarded to work on IFAD sponsored "Filling the Inter-Generational Gap in Knowledge on Agricultural Water Management: twinning Junior and Senior Experts." Also was nominated as a change agent by USAID-Ethiopia. Driven by his passion, he has published more than five books on Amazon, sharing his knowledge and insights with a broader audience.

For inquiries, use email:
mast962004@yahoo.com

Books are available with the link:
amazon.com/author/mastewalademe

9 798345 066911